GUITAR • VOCAL

LENNY KRAVITZ
GREATEST HITS

Cover photography by Mark Seliger

ISBN 978-1-57560-455-8

Visit our website at
www.cherrylane.com

LENNY KRAVITZ
GREATEST HITS

There couldn't be a more perfect time to catch up to the remarkable career of Lenny Kravitz. After two consecutive Grammy Awards, a pair of huge hit singles in "Fly Away," and his cover of Guess Who's "American Woman"—both from his biggest album to date, the triple-platinum *5*—the rock superstar is at the peak of his popularity and artistic power.

With his brand-new *Greatest Hits* album on Virgin Records America, Kravitz brings into sharp relief his multiple talents as a writer, producer, arranger, guitarist, multi-instrumentalist, and live performer.

The record offers a retrospective of Kravitz's decade-plus output—touching on his eclectic palette of rock, funk, jazz, soul, R & B, country, reggae, blues, gospel, pop, techno, psychedelic, and classical influences—following in the footsteps of a personal pantheon which includes James Brown, Jimi Hendrix, Led Zeppelin, and Bob Marley. The record boasts 14 "greatest hits" plus one brand-new track, "Again," recorded recently in his home Roxie Studios in Miami, named after his late mother, TV star Roxie Roker.

The songs range from his 1989 debut album, *Let Love Rule*—with the title track trumpeting his belief in classic '60s rock ideals—to his 1998 effort, *5*—which sold more than six million copies worldwide, remaining on the *Billboard* charts for more than 110 consecutive weeks. "Fly Away" and "American Woman" earned Kravitz two consecutive Grammys as Best Rock Vocal Performance Male, while the former made history by topping the *Billboard* rock charts in three different Rock formats the same week.

The record's highlights include commercial successes such as the #2-charting 1991 breakthrough "It Ain't Over 'Til It's Over" (from *Mama Said*), and his Top 15 U.S. single "Are You Gonna Go My Way" (from the 1993 double-platinum album of the same name)—which earned him a '93 MTV Video Music Award for Best Male Video. There are also fan favorites like the tongue-in-cheek anthem "Rock and Roll Is Dead" (from '95's *Circus*) and the electronica-tinged "Black Velveteen," one of the overlooked cuts from the smash *5* album.

This compilation drives home the remarkable fact that Kravitz has played and arranged virtually every note on his five albums. "I think I've covered a lot of ground," he says. "There are a lot of different elements in my music, and this really shows where I've been and where I'm going, as well."

Kravitz's track record bears testament to those abilities. He's co-written a #1 song for Madonna ("Justify My Love"), recorded with Mick Jagger (a version of Bill Withers' "Use Me" for the Stones singer's 1993 solo album, *Wandering Spirit*) and Sean and Yoko Ono (a version of "Give Peace a Chance"), collaborated with Aerosmith ("Line Up" on the band's *Get A Grip* album), worked with both Al Green and Curtis Mayfield, produced records for Cree Summer, and contributed tracks to tribute albums for both Kiss and Mayfield. He's also a legendary live performer who has consistently toured the world, and a recording artist who has outlasted virtually all of his contemporaries.

"It's a blessing for me to have the opportunity to put this record out, especially in an era of music when careers are very disposable," says Kravitz.

Usually, a Greatest Hits collection comes at the end of an artist's career. For Lenny, it marks a new beginning, a fresh start after eleven years as a recording artist. One decade down, and plenty more to go.

"Doing this record brought back a lot of memories," says Lenny. "You remember what you were going through at the time you wrote and recorded each song. It also recalled the work process. It's like having these old friends drop by that you haven't seen in a long time. You don't remember all the details, but you feel good about them."

"I'm not about to stop making music," says Kravitz. "In fact, I feel like I'm at the beginning of my career."

Greatest Hits gives those legions of new fans who have been turned on to Lenny Kravitz through "Fly Away" and "American Woman" a chance to catch up with what he's been up to for the past 11 years, while offering his long-time audience the songs he's best known for. And it sets the stage for the next act in Lenny Kravitz's still-rising output.

"I'm looking forward to the next album now," he says. "I feel I'm still growing as an artist."

Greatest Hits offers conclusive proof of that.

ABOUT THE SONGS
A SELECTED COMMENTARY

by Lenny Kravitz

AGAIN

I was in a studio starting to record a sixth album. All of a sudden this song came out of me, and right about that time we began to discuss doing a Greatest Hits album. Out of all the stuff I'd recorded, that was the newest and I thought most appropriate to stand on its own. It kind of felt like it wasn't meant for the next studio album. I felt it would be cool for this album because it's very "sing-along-y." Very simple. But with a lot of feeling. A song for everybody. I recorded it five times before I was happy with it.

AMERICAN WOMAN

I cut it in a day. I always loved the song; the vocal was genius. I just wanted to make it funkier. Not that the original isn't completely funky. It's funny because, as far as the production goes, there's no snare drum in that song. It's just claps, kick drums, and hi-hats. So I broke it down, and somehow, by breaking it down, it became funkier. If you listen to a lot of old funk records, the drums are really small. But you don't perceive it like that because the groove is so heavy.

FLY AWAY

This wasn't even going to be on the album. I had finished 5 and I was at the studio one day trying out this guitar and amp. I was just jamming and I started to play the chords. I started playing this riff because the guitar sounded chunky in that register. And I thought it was kind of cool. I started cutting it, and about an hour later I had a completed track. I thought it could be a b-side until a friend of mine, an architect, told me it was a hit. I thought it was a real simple throwaway because it came out so quickly. He begged me to put it on the record. So I called L.A., stopped the pressing and added the song. And that was it. The people at the label said it would never get on rock radio.

BLACK VELVETEEN

I put rock together with techno because I felt it was appropriate for the song. If it's right for the song, I'll do anything.

LET LOVE RULE

When that came out, people thought I was being naïve, but there are a lot of cynical people, y'know. I was just stating how it is. If that makes me naïve, than Bob Marley was naïve when he sang, "Don't worry 'bout a thing/Every little thing is gonna be alright." I was just putting it in a simple form. Ultimately, no matter how hip and sophisticated we all try to be, the bottom line is we all just want to be loved, to feel love.

IT AIN'T OVER 'TIL IT'S OVER

It was just amazing to me that, all of a sudden, I was hearing my music on the radio and coming out of cars.

ARE YOU GONNA GO MY WAY

That song busted me out as far as people's perceptions of me. And it was completely unexpected. It's another one of those songs written in a day on a paper bag. Who knew? I had no idea.

ROCK AND ROLL IS DEAD

That song was completely misunderstood. I was sort of portrayed as this guy who's helping to save rock 'n' roll and all of a sudden I'm saying it's dead. What did I mean by saying that? A lot of people don't take it that one layer deeper. They hear the title and chorus and take it at face value. They think I'm being serious when actually I'm a very big clown—but you have to know me to see that. I'm constantly cracking up and cracking up everybody else around me. They see my photos and think I labor over my image and I'm this cool, brooding artist. But I'm just having fun with it.

ARE YOU GONNA GO MY WAY

Words by Lenny Kravitz

Music by Lenny Kravitz
and Craig Ross

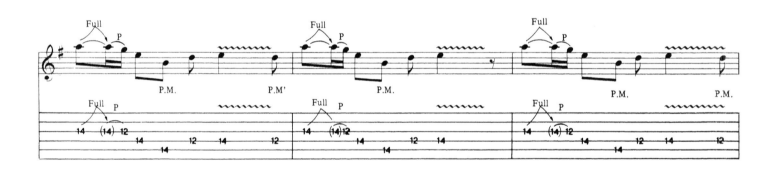

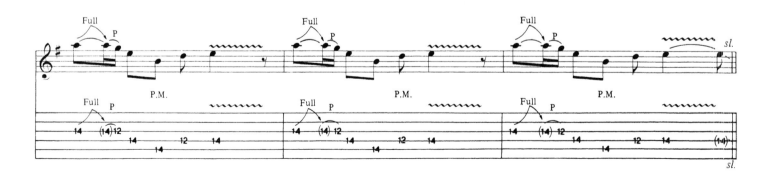

1st, 2nd Verses
w/Riff A (1st bar only) (8 times)
N.C.(E5)

1. I was born_____ long a - go. I'm the cho-sen, I'm the one.
2. *See additional lyrics*

I have come_____ to save the day. And I won't leave un-til I'm done.

(G5)

2nd time substitute Rhy. Fill 1
(Gtr. II only)

So that's why_____ you got to try. You got to breathe and have some fun.

Gtr. II

Full
P

(Gtr. II out)

P.M.

Full
P

17 (17) 15
17 15 17
17

17 17 ✕ 15 ✕ 14 ✕ 15 ✕ 17 17

Gtr. I

Full
P

Full
P

5 (5) 3
5 3 5
3

5 5 ✕ 4 ✕ 3 ✕ 2 ✕ 4

w/Riff A (1st bar only) (4 times)
(E5)

Though I'm not paid,_____ I play this game. And I won't stop un-til I'm done.

Rhy. Fill 1

(Gtr. II out)

17 17 16 16 ✕ 15 ✕ 14 16 16 16 16

9

*With one vol. knob set to zero, flick toggle
switch back and forth in specified rhythm.

Additional Lyrics

2. I don't know why we always cry.
   This we must leave and get undone.
   We must engage and rearrange.
   And turn this planet back to one.
   So tell me why we got to die
   And kill each other one by one.
   We've got to love and rub-a-dub.
   We've got to dance and be in love.
   But what I really want to know is... *etc.*

FLY AWAY

Words and Music by
Lenny Kravitz

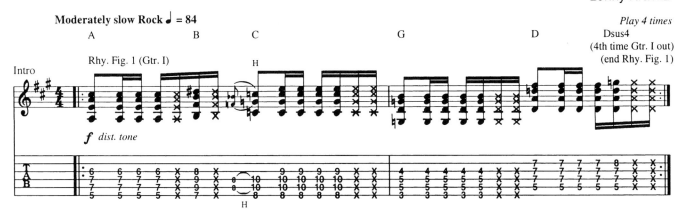

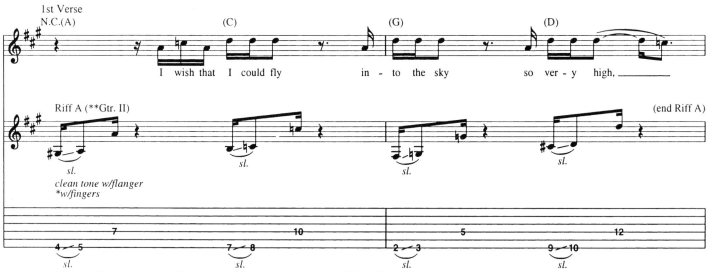

*Notes on 6th stg. are played w/R.H. thumb; notes on 4th stg. are snapped w/R.H. middle finger.

**Bass arr. for gtr.

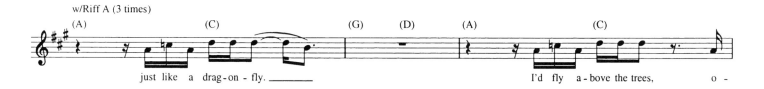

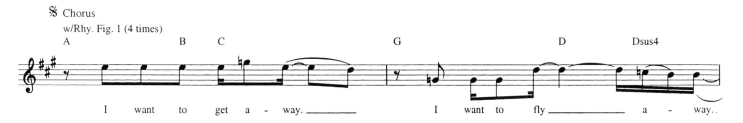

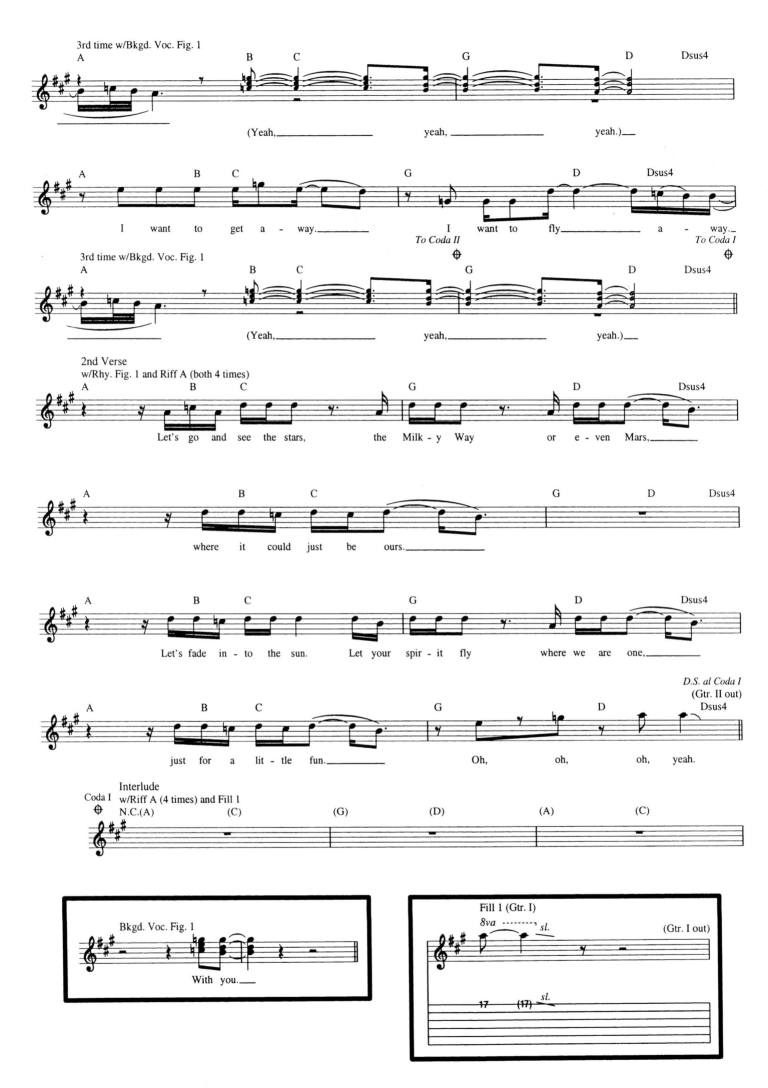

(Spoken:) I got-ta get a-way.   Girl, I got-ta

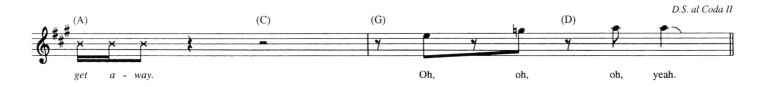

D.S. al Coda II

get a-way.   Oh,   oh,   oh,   yeah.

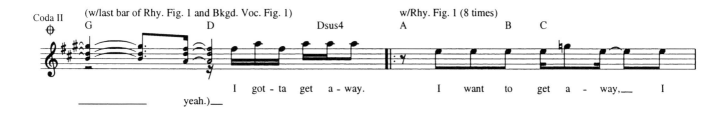

Coda II

(w/last bar of Rhy. Fig. 1 and Bkgd. Voc. Fig. 1)   w/Rhy. Fig. 1 (8 times)

_____   yeah.)__   I got-ta get a-way.   I   want   to   get a - way,__   I

want   to   get a - way.__   I   want   to   get a - way,__   I

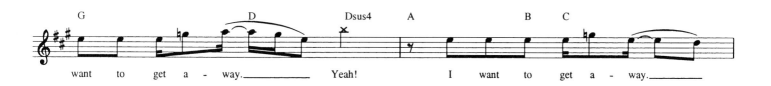

want   to   get a - way.__   Yeah!   I   want   to   get a - way.__

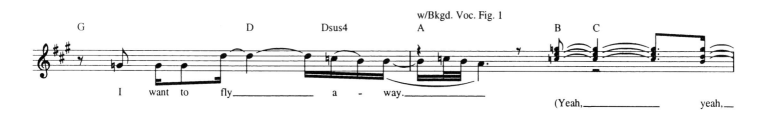

w/Bkgd. Voc. Fig. 1

I   want   to   fly__   a - way.__   (Yeah,_____   yeah,__

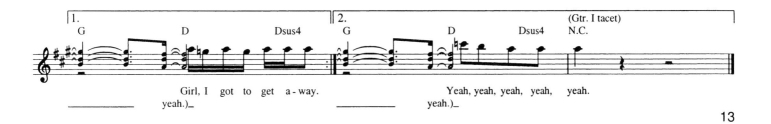

1.   2.   (Gtr. I tacet)

Girl, I got to get a-way.   Yeah, yeah, yeah, yeah,   yeah.
_____   yeah.)__   _____   yeah.)__

ROCK AND ROLL IS DEAD

Words and Music by
Lenny Kravitz

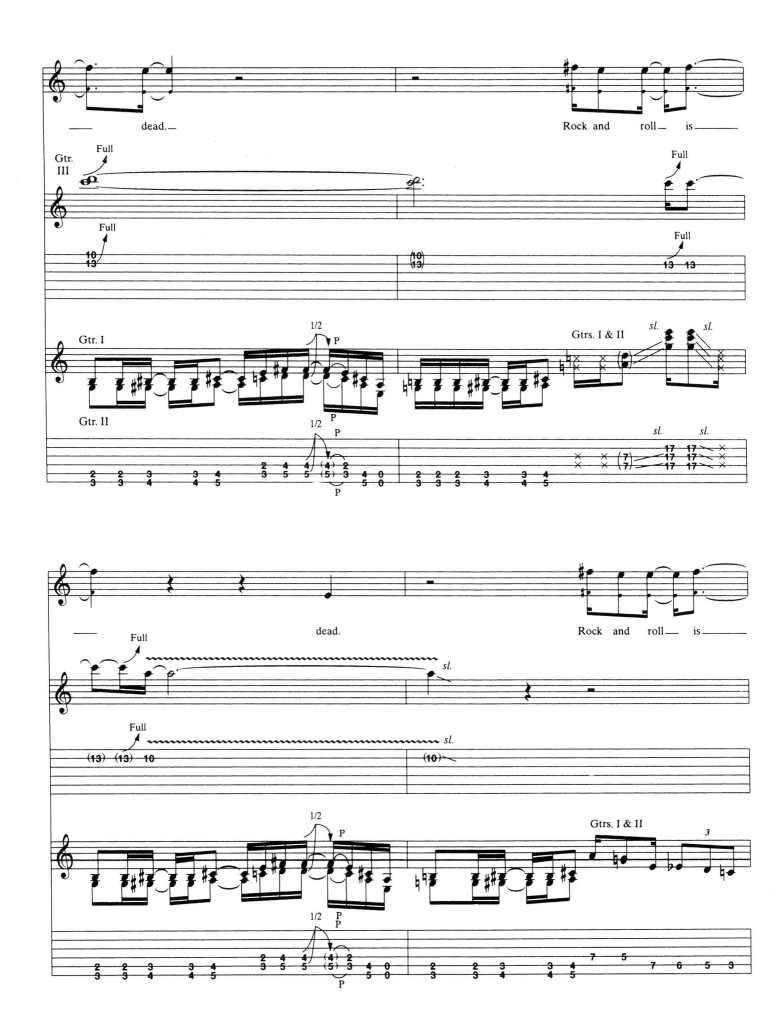

dead.

Rock and roll— is—

Gtr. III

Full

Full

Full

Full

Gtr. I

1/2

P

Gtrs. I & II

Gtr. II

1/2

P

sl.

sl.

dead.

Rock and roll— is—

Full

sl.

Full

sl.

1/2

P

Gtrs. I & II

1/2

P

P

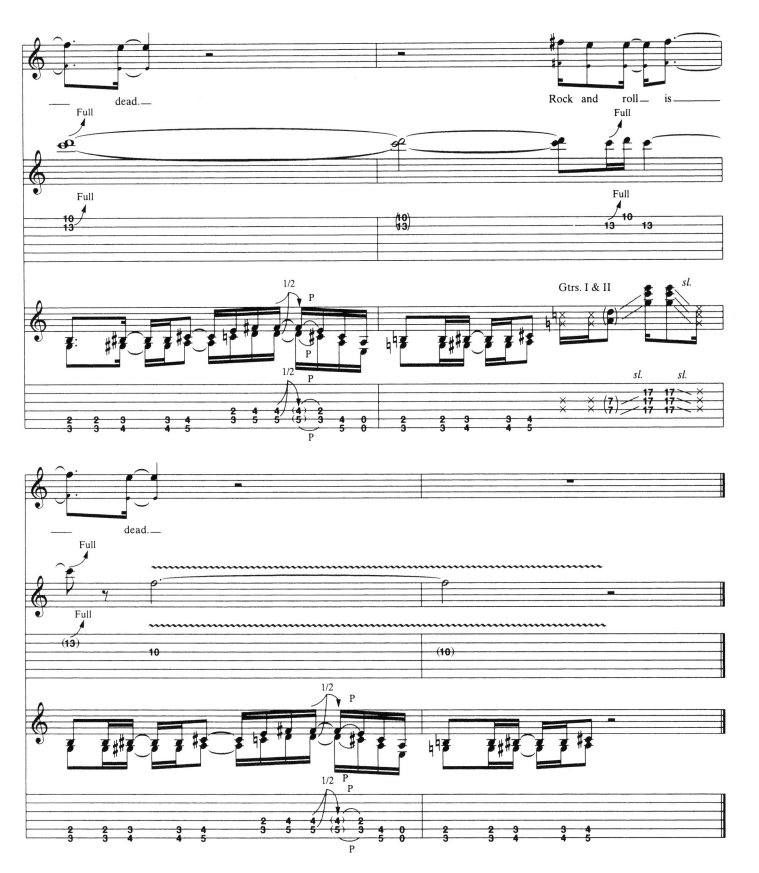

Additional Lyrics

2. You can't even sing or play an instrument
   So you just scream instead. Ooh, yeah!
   You're livin' for an image
   So you got five hundred women in your bed. Ooh, yeah!
   Rock and roll is dead.
   But it's real hard to be yourself
   When you're livin' with those demons in your head. Ooh, yeah! *(To Chorus)*

AGAIN

Words and Music by
Lenny Kravitz

ev - er see you a - gain. _ _ev - er see you a - gain._ I've al - ways known

(Through time that

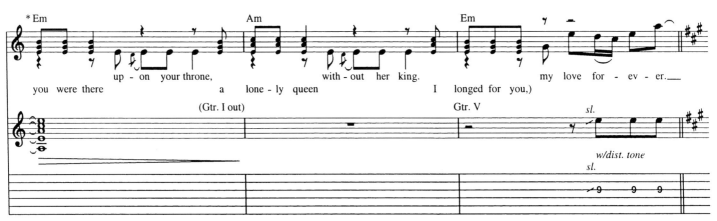

you were there a - lone - ly queen I longed for you,)

up - on your throne, with - out her king. my love for - ev - er._

*Chords implied by bkgd. voc. (next 3 bars)

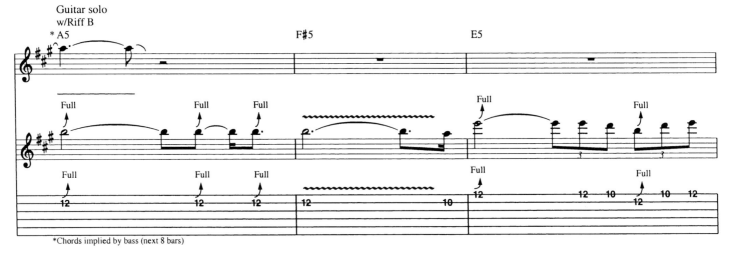

Guitar solo
w/Riff B

*Chords implied by bass (next 8 bars)

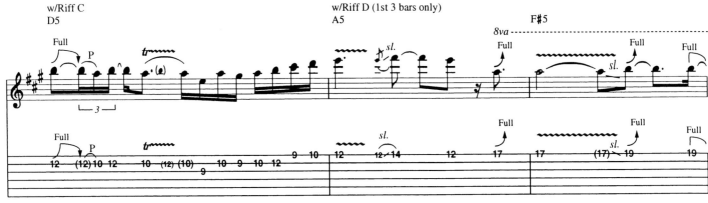

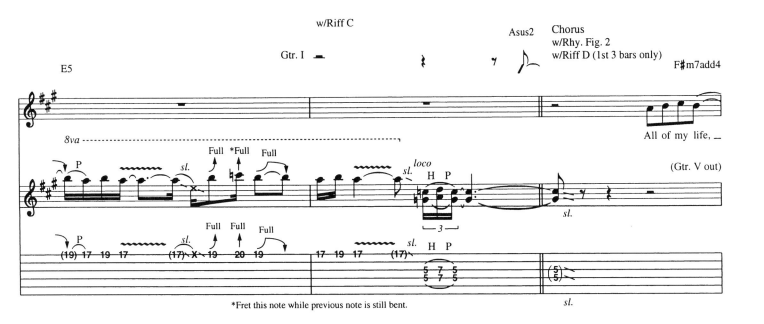

*Fret this note while previous note is still bent.

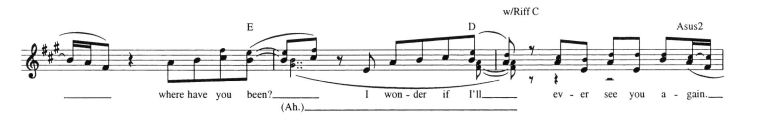

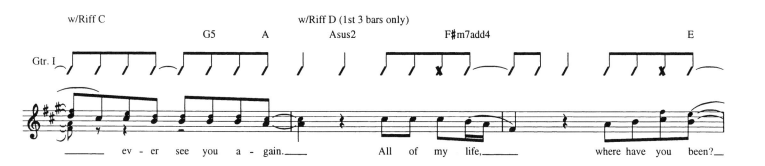

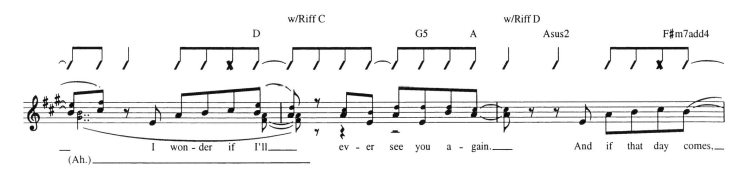

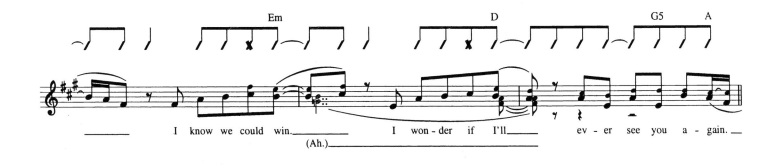

I know we could win._____ I won - der if I'll_____ ev - er see you a - gain.____

(Ah.)_____

Outro
A

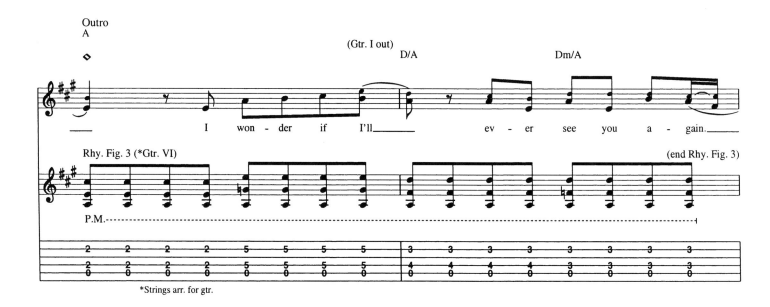

(Gtr. I out)
D/A   Dm/A

I won - der if I'll_____ ev - er see you a - gain.

Rhy. Fig. 3 (*Gtr. VI)   (end Rhy. Fig. 3)

P.M.

*Strings arr. for gtr.

w/Rhy. Fig. 3 (4 times)
A   A7(no3rd)   D/A   Dm/A

I won - der if I'll_____ ev - er see you a - gain._____

A   A7(no3rd)   D/A   Dm/A   A   A7(no3rd)

Begin fade

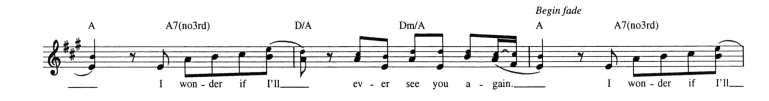

I won - der if I'll_____ ev - er see you a - gain._____ I won - der if I'll_____

G5   A   (Gtr. I out)   Fade out
                                             D/A   Dm/A

Gtr. I

ev - er see you a - gain._____ I won - der if I'll_____ ev - er see you a - gain._____

IT AIN'T OVER 'TIL IT'S OVER

Words and Music by
Lenny Kravitz

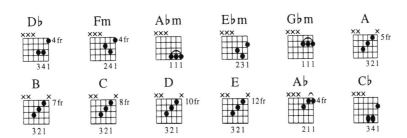

Light Funk ♩ =84

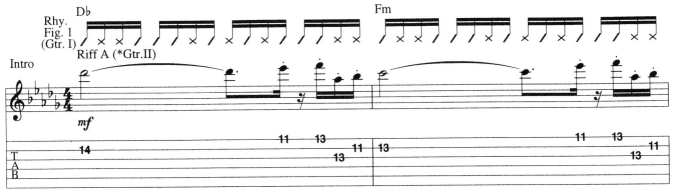

*Strings arr. for gtr.

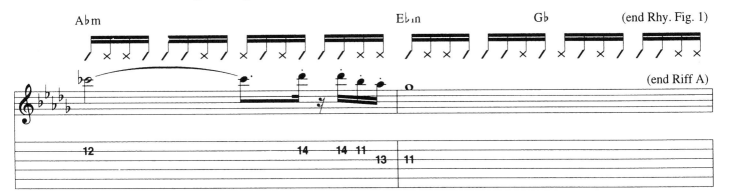

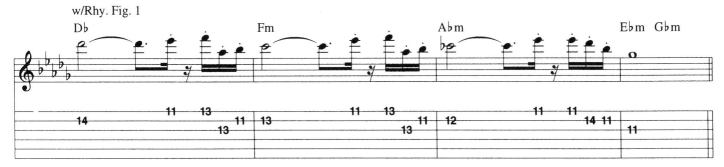

Here _ we are __ still to geth - er. We are one.

So _ much time _ wast - ed __ play - ing games with love.

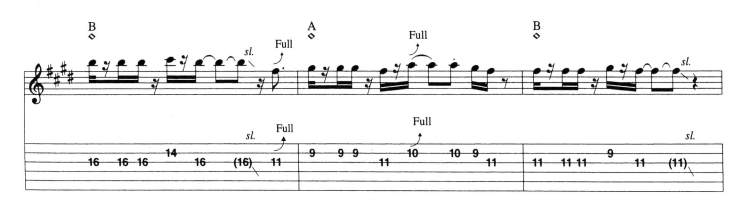

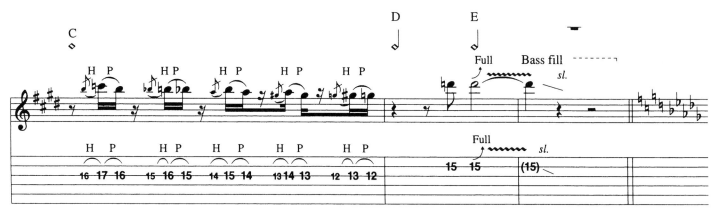

Chorus

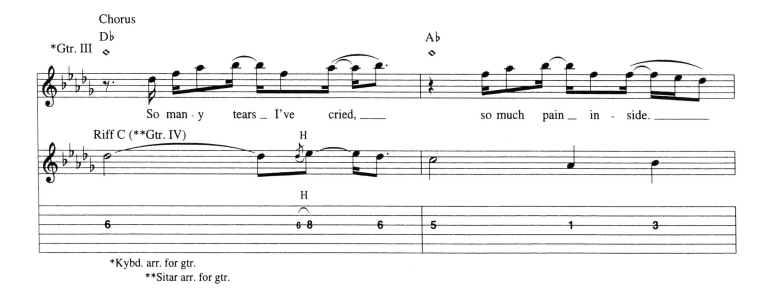

So man-y tears _ I've cried, _____ so much pain _ in - side. _____

*Kybd. arr. for gtr.
**Sitar arr. for gtr.

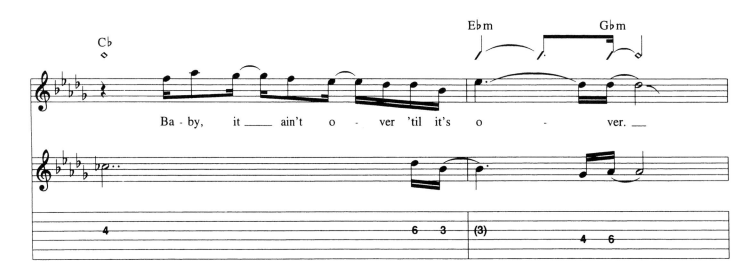

Ba - by, it _____ ain't o - ver 'til it's o - ver. ___

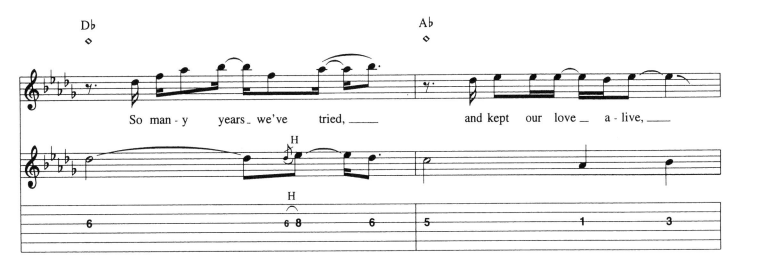

So man-y years we've tried, _____ and kept our love a-live, _____

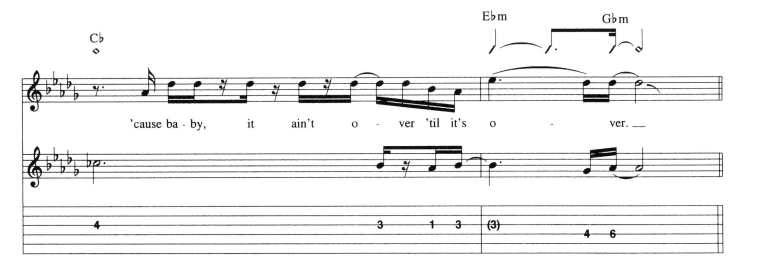

'cause ba-by, it ain't o - ver 'til it's o - ver. _____

w/Rhy. Fig. 1 (2 times) and Riffs A & C

So man-y tears I've cried, _____ so much pain - in - side, _____

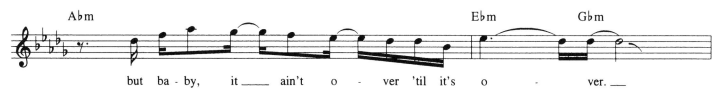

but ba-by, it _____ ain't o - ver 'til it's o - ver. _____

w/Riff B

So _____ man-y years _____ we've _____ tried _____ to keep our love _____ a - live, _____

Repeat ad lib and fade

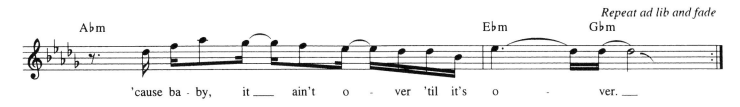

'cause ba-by, it _____ ain't o - ver 'til it's o - ver. _____

CAN'T GET YOU OFF MY MIND

Words and Music by
Lenny Kravitz

*Play all rhy. figs. w/slight variations ad lib when recalled (throughout).
**12-stg. acous.

1st Verse
w/Rhy. Fig. 1A (2 times)

Life is just a lone-ly high-way, I'm out here on the o-pen road.

30

Copyright © 1995 Miss Bessie Music (ASCAP)
International Copyright Secured All Rights Reserved

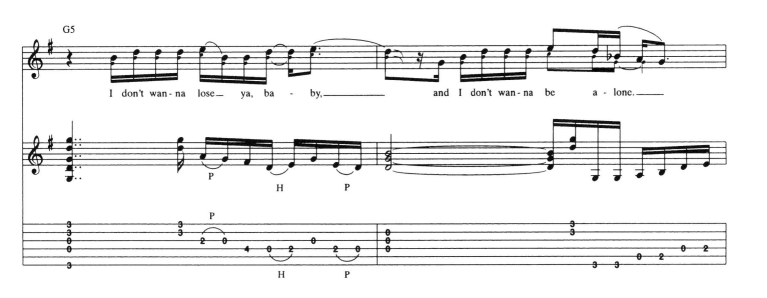

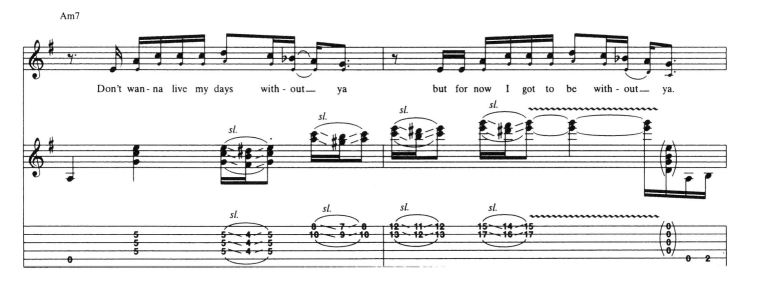

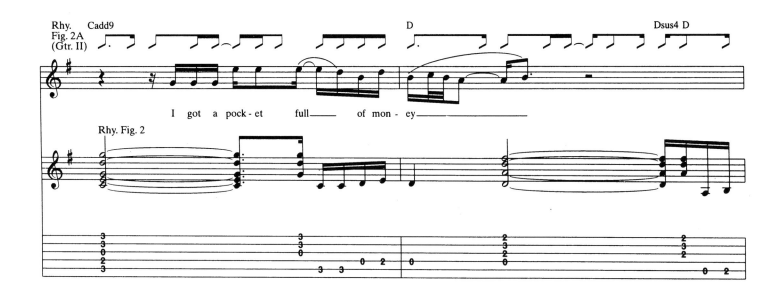

I got a pock-et full____ of mon-ey____

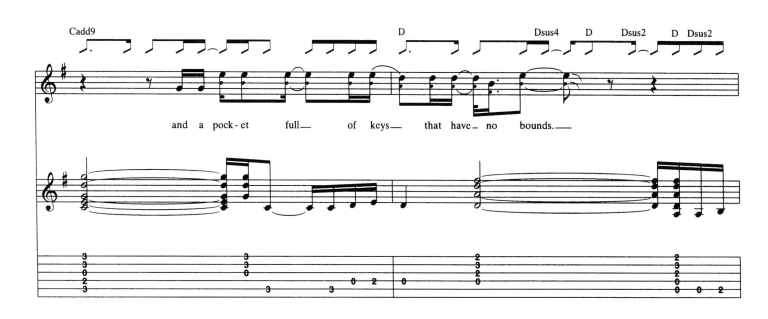

and a pock-et full____ of keys____ that have____ no bounds.____

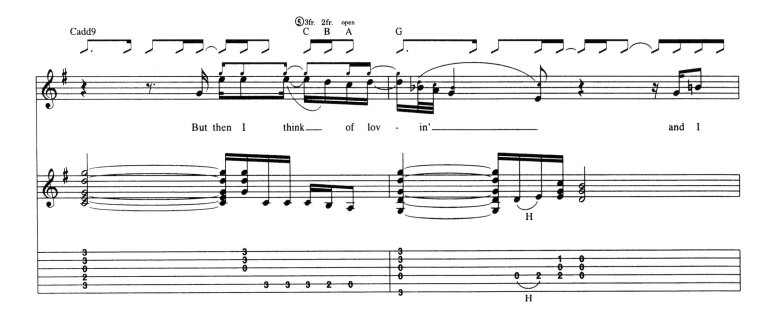

But then I think____ of lov - in'_____ and I

*Beginning at beat 3, an elec. 12-stg. enters and comes in and out while doubling portions of Gtr. I's parts (till end).

that this is kill-in' me? I don't wan-na push— ya, ba — by,———

Rhy. Fig. 3

— and I don't want ya to be told.——— It's just that I can't breathe with-out— ya,
(end Rhy. Fig. 3)

*Omit during verse.
Include only when Rhy. Fig. 3
is recalled during solo.

feel like I'm gon-na lose con-trol.—— I got a pock-et full——— of mon-

ey,_____ oh, yes I do, and a pock - et full of keys____

_____ that have_ no bounds.____ But when it comes____ to lov -

in',_____ I just can't get you off__ of my

mind,_____ yeah._____ Am I a fool__

Bridge

__ to think_ that there's a lit - tle hope? Yeah,_____ yeah,____ yeah.
(Ah,_____ ah, ah,____

Tell me, ba - by. Yeah.__ What are the rules,__
ah.

__ the rea - sons and the do's and dont's? Yeah,_____ yeah,____ yeah.
Ah, ah, ah.)____

Tell me, ba - by.   Tell me, ba -

by,   yeah,   what do you   feel   in - side?

Guitar solo
w/Rhy. Figs. 1 & 1A (2 times)

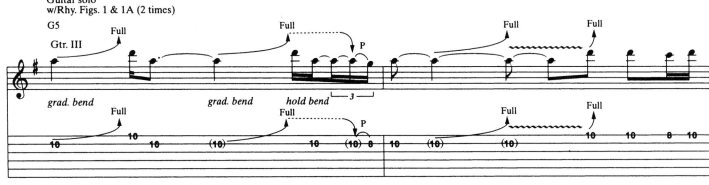

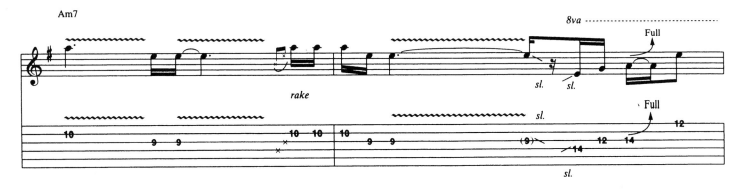

36

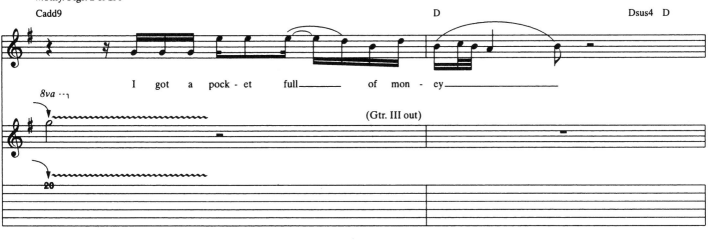

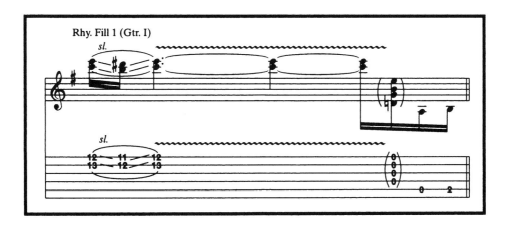

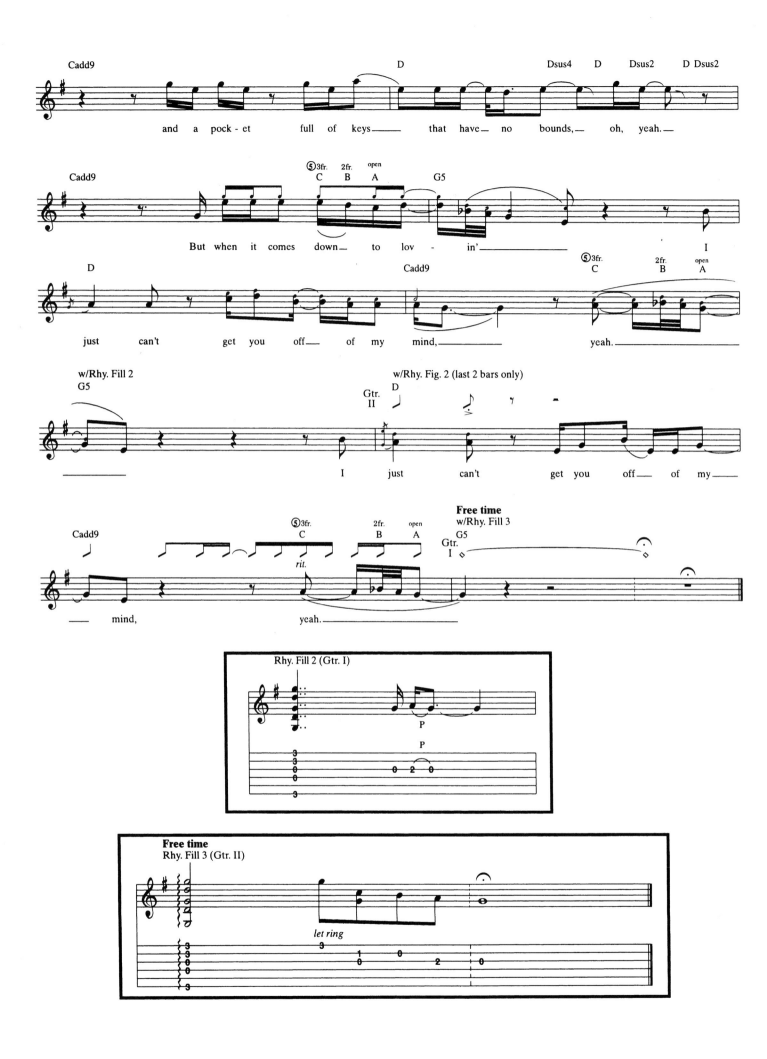

MR. CAB DRIVER

Words and Music by
Lenny Kravitz

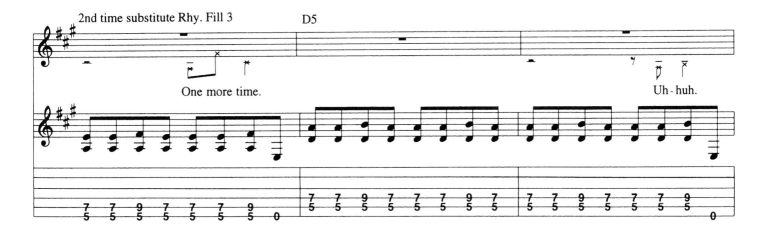

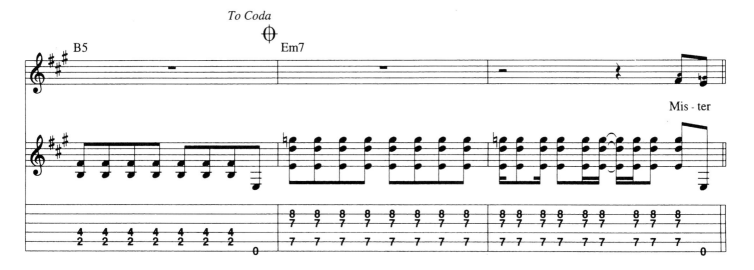

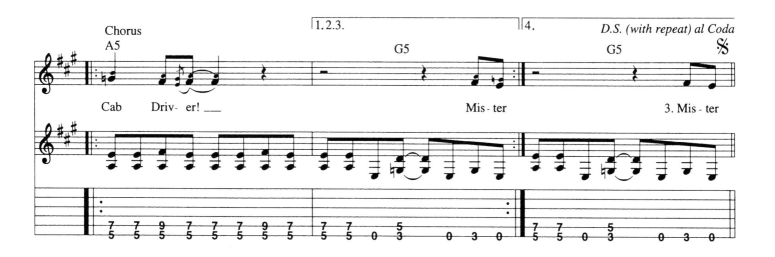

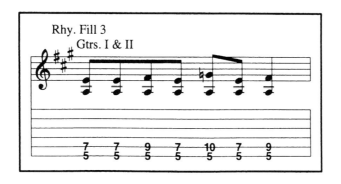

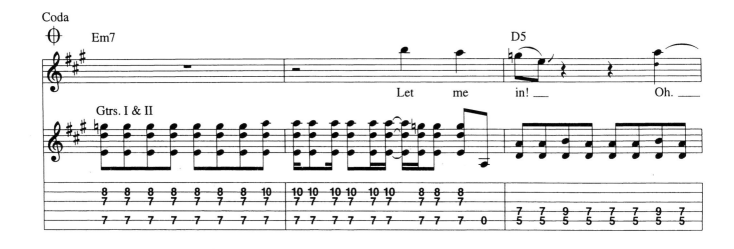

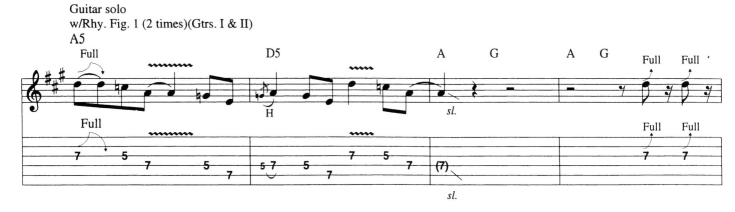

Additional Lyrics

2. Mr. Cab Driver won't stop to pick me up.
   Mr. Cab Driver I might need some help.
   Mr. Cab Driver only thinks about himself.

3. Mr. Cab Driver don't like the way I look.
   He don't like dreads. He thinks we're all crooks.
   Mr. Cab Driver reads too many storybooks.

4. Mr. Cab Driver pass me up with eyes of fire.
   Mr. Cab Driver thinks we're all 165'ers.
   Mr. Cab Driver, fuck you. I'm a surviver.

AMERICAN WOMAN

Written by Burton Cummings,
Randy Bachman, Gary Peterson and Jim Kale

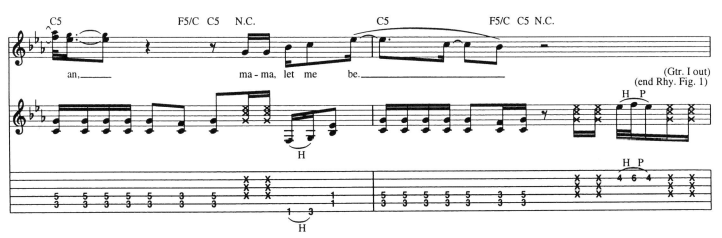

Don't come hang-ing 'round_ my door._ I don't want to see your face__ no more._ I

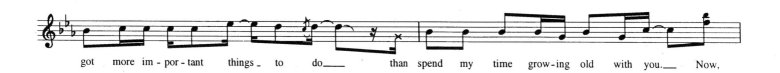

got more im-por-tant things_ to do___ than spend my time grow-ing old with you.__ Now,

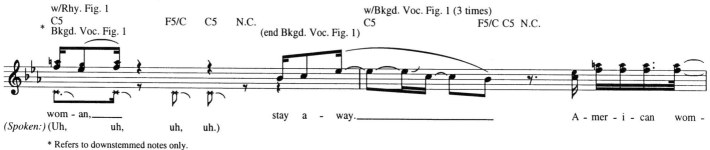

w/Rhy. Fig. 1
* C5　　　　　　F5/C　C5　N.C.　　　　　　　w/Bkgd. Voc. Fig. 1 (3 times)
* Bkgd. Voc. Fig. 1　　　　　　　　　(end Bkgd. Voc. Fig. 1)　C5　　　　　F5/C C5 N.C.

wom - an,____ stay a - way._____ A - mer - i - can wom-
(Spoken:) (Uh, uh, uh, uh.)

* Refers to downstemmed notes only.

C5　　　　　　　　　F5/C　C5　N.C.　　　　　　　　C5　　　　　　F5/C C5 N.C.
(Gtr. I out)

an_____ lis - ten what I say._____

Bb5 C5　　　　　Bb5　　C5　　　　　Bb5 C5　　　　　Bb5　　C5　　　　　N.C.
Bkgd. Voc. Fig. 2　　　　　　　　　　　　　　　　　　　　　　　　　(end Bkgd. Voc. Fig. 2)

(Bow,_ ka, dow,_ ka, dow,_ ka, dow, dow. Bow,_ ka, dow,_ ka, dow,_ ka, dow, dow.)

Rhy. Fig. 2 (Gtr. II)

Rhy. Fig. 2A (Gtr. III)

STAND BY MY WOMAN

Words by Lenny Kravitz

Music by Lenny Kravitz, Henry Hirsch,
Stephen Pasch and Anthony Krizan

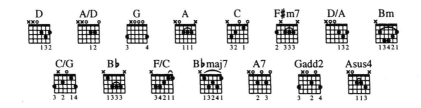

Oh, there were times__ I was-n't kind.__

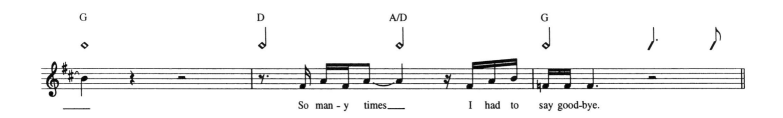

And there were times__ I was-n't e-ven 'round.   And there were times__ I made you cry.__

So man-y times__ I had to say good-bye.

Pre-chorus

When you want to talk, I'm on the phone.__ But now,__
But, ba-by, now I'm here for you, 'cause__

ba - by,__ yeah,__ I am here__ for you a - lone.__ I'm gon-na
ba - by,__ yeah,__ I am so__ in love with you.__

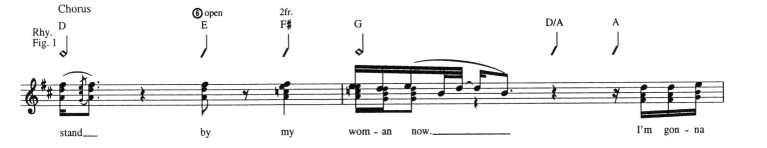

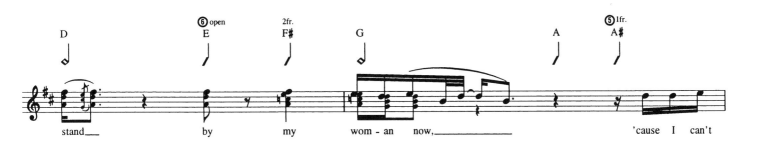

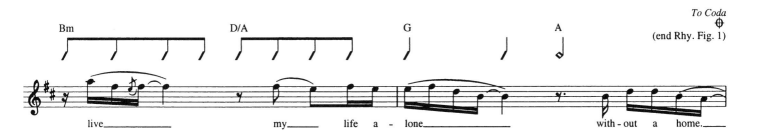

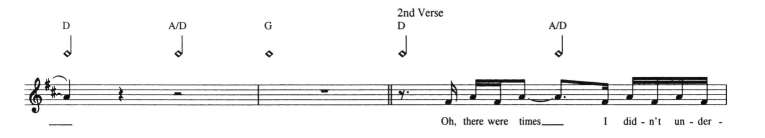

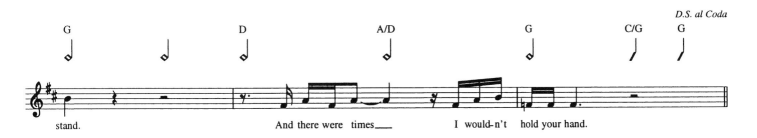

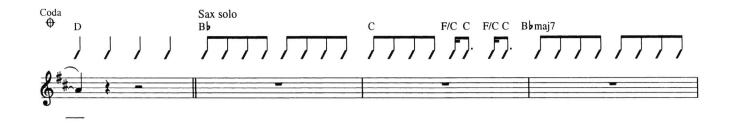

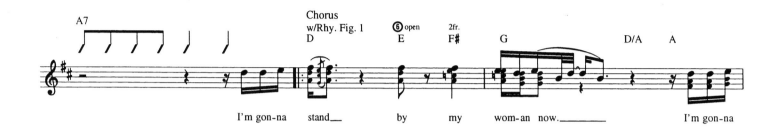

I'm gon-na stand___ by my wom-an now._____ I'm gon-na

stand_ by my wom-an now,_____ 'cause_ I can't live_____ my___ life a-

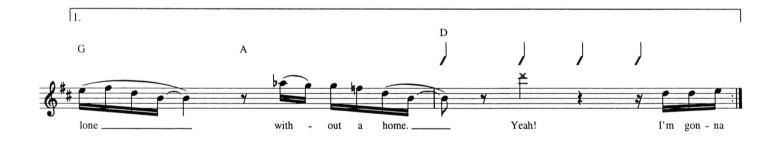

lone _____ with - out a home._____ Yeah! I'm gon-na

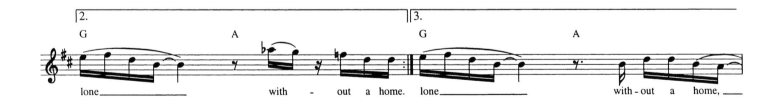

lone_____ with - out a home. lone_____ with-out a home,___

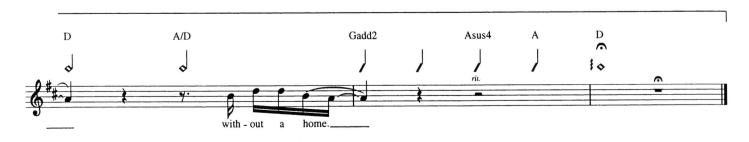

with - out a home._____

ALWAYS ON THE RUN

Words by Lenny Kravitz
Music by Lenny Kravitz and Slash

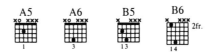

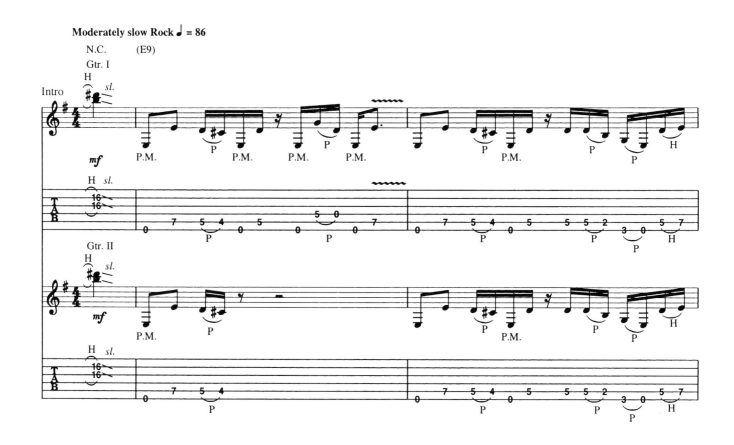

*Played by Gtr. II when recalled, throughout. Play all guitar figures w/slight variations ad lib when repeated or recalled (throughout).

55

Rhy. Fig. 1 (end Rhy. Fig. 1)

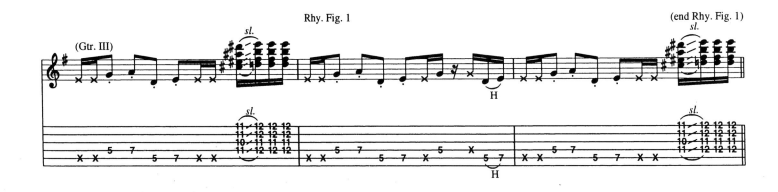

1st Verse
w/Riff A and Rhy. Fig. 1 (both 2 times)
N.C.(E9)

1. And my ma-ma said   that your__ life__ is a gift.__   And my ma-ma said,   "There's much__

(1st), 2nd, 3rd Verses
w/Riff A (3½ times) and Rhy. Fig. 1 (4 times)
N.C.(E9)

__ weight   you will lift."__   And my ma-ma said,   "Leave those__ bad__ boys a-lone."__
2.3. *See additional lyrics*

Gtr. II substitute Rhy. Fill 1

And my ma-ma said,   "Be home__ be-fore dawn."__   And my ma-ma said,   "You can

(resume Riff A)   3rd time Gtr. II substitute Rhy. Fill 1   3rd time Gtr. II substitute last bar of Riff A

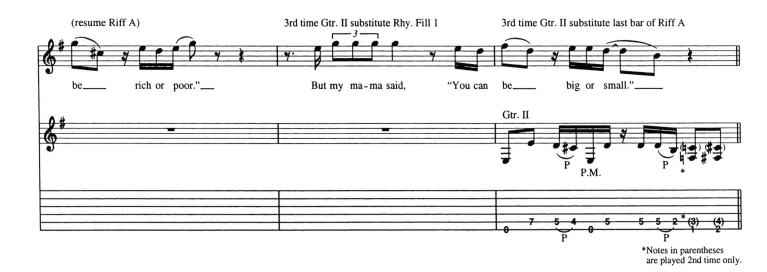

be__   rich or poor."__   But my ma-ma said,   "You can be__ big or small."__

Gtr. II

*Notes in parentheses
are played 2nd time only.

Rhy. Fill 1 (Gtr. II)

56

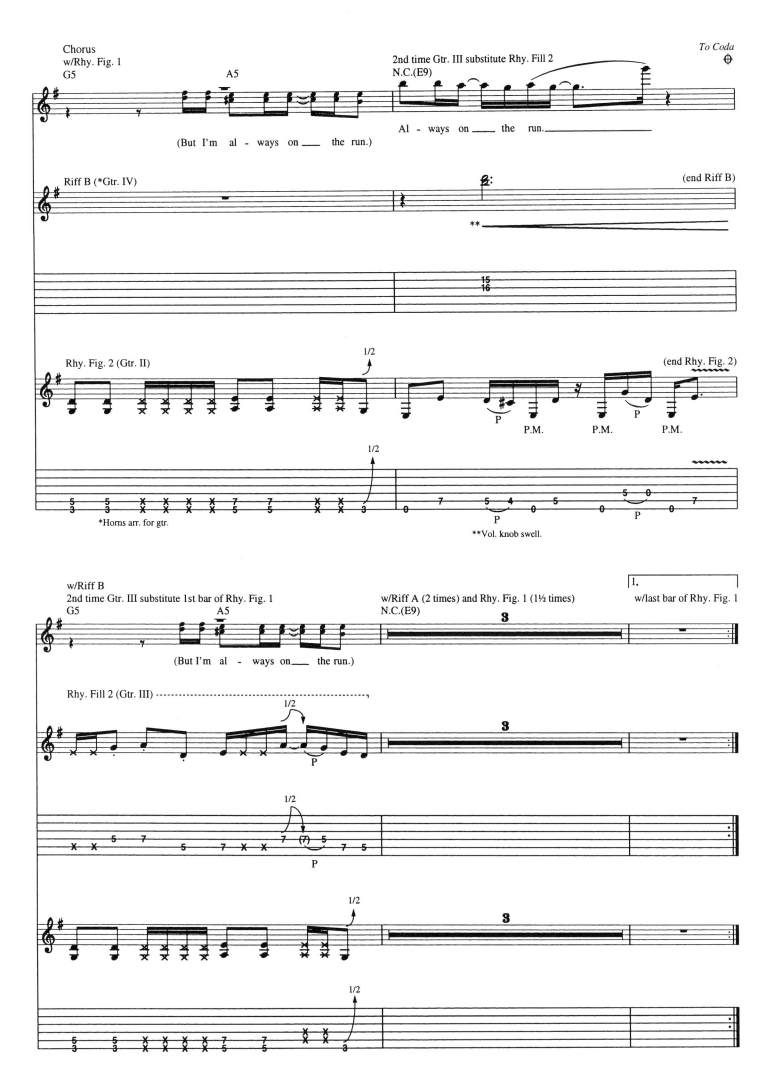

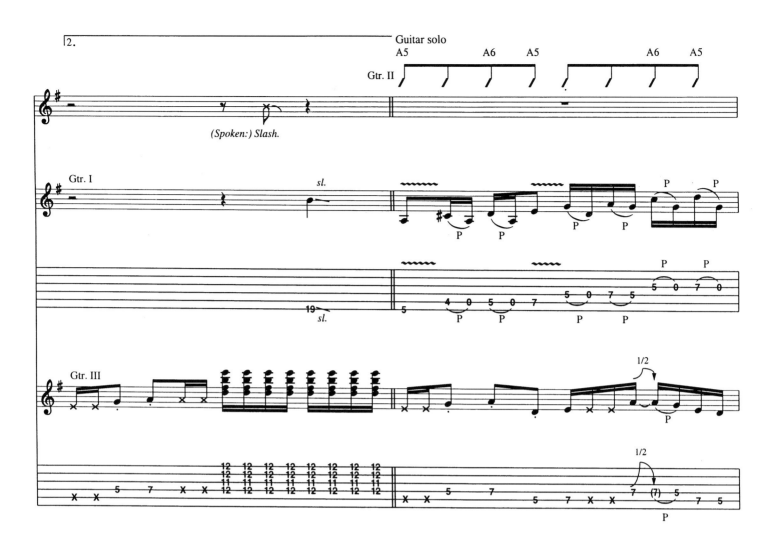

(Spoken:) Slash.

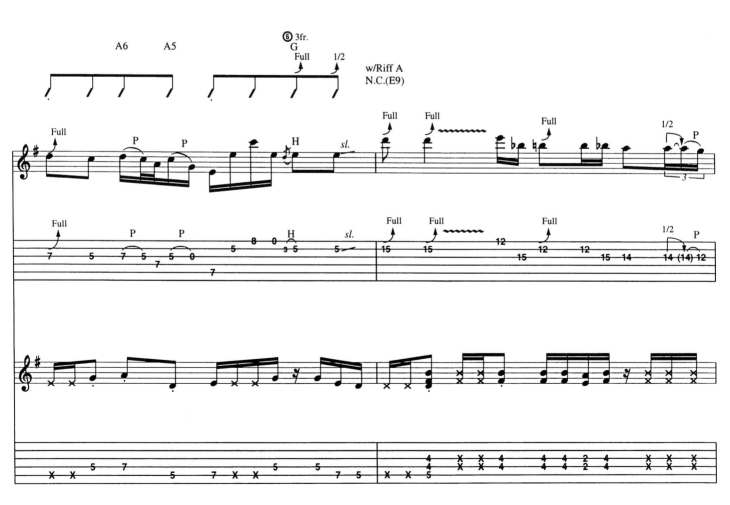

Coda

w/Rhy. Fig. 2 (2½ times) and Riff B (2 times)
w/Rhy. Fill 2
G5   A5   w/1st bar of Rhy. Fig. 1
                                                                                        N.C.(E9)

On   the   run._____

(But   I'm   al - ways   on_____   the   run.)

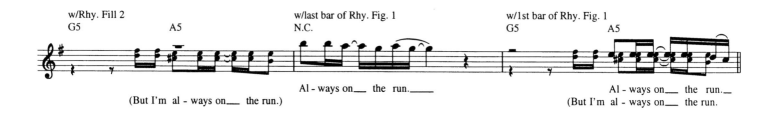

w/Rhy. Fill 2
G5   A5   w/last bar of Rhy. Fig. 1   w/1st bar of Rhy. Fig. 1
                                                N.C.   G5   A5

Al - ways on__ the run._____

(But I'm al - ways on__ the run.)   Al - ways on__ the run.
                                                                                  (But I'm al - ways on__ the run.

Outro
w/Riff A (2 times) and Rhy. Fig. 1 (6½ times)
N.C.(E9)

(Spoken:)   Uh,   what's up, ma-ma?   You want it,   uh,   right now?

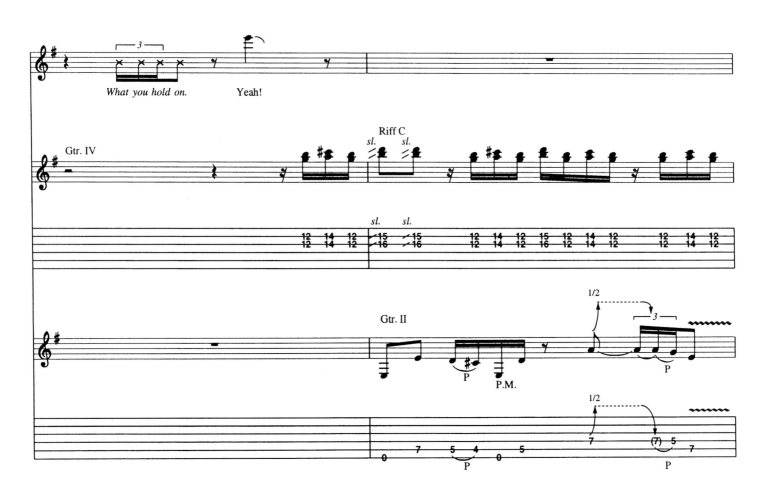

What you hold on.   Yeah!

Gtr. IV

Riff C

Gtr. II

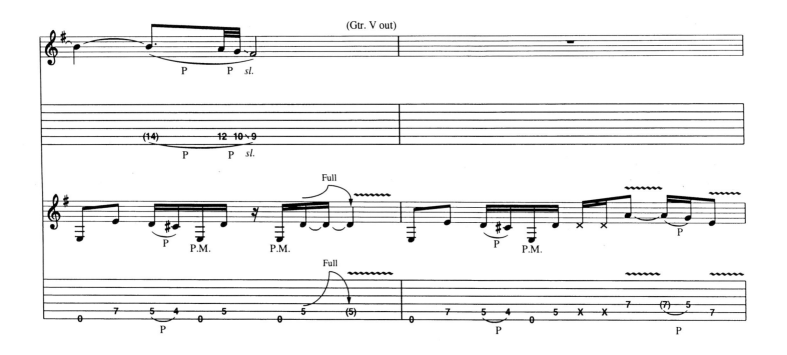

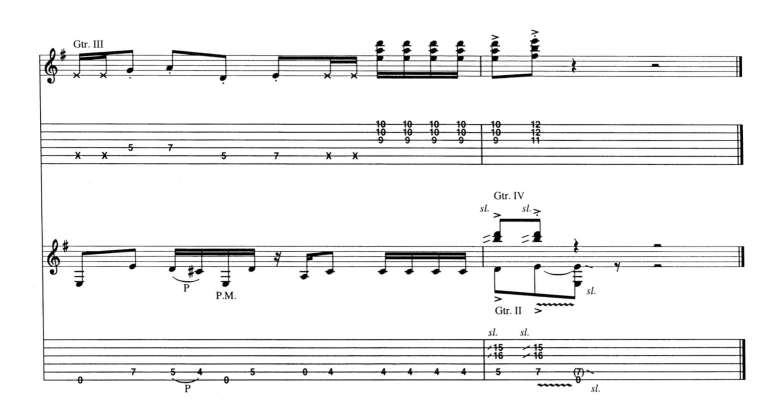

Additional Lyrics

2. And my mama said that it's good to be fruitful.
   But my mama said, "Don't take more than a mouthful."
   And my mama said that it's good to be natural.
   And my mama said that it's good to be factual. *(To Chorus)*

3. And my mama said, "Baby, don't ride that crazy horse."
   And my mama said, "You must push with much force."
   And my mama said, "Go get all that you're after."
   And my mama said that love's all that matters. *(To Chorus)*

HEAVEN HELP

Words and Music by
Gerry DeVeaux and Terry Britten

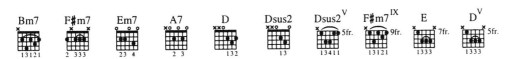

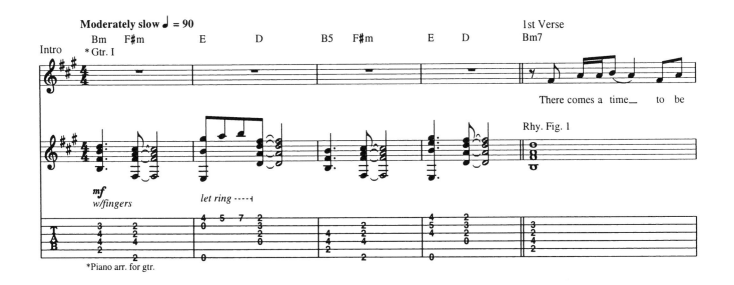

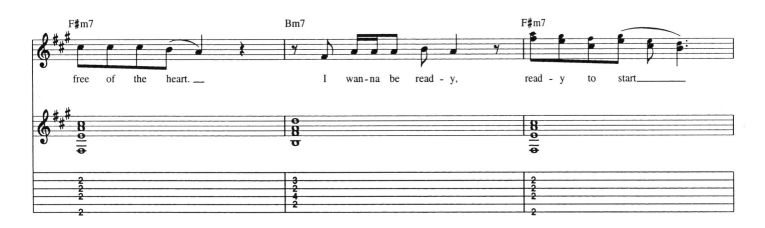

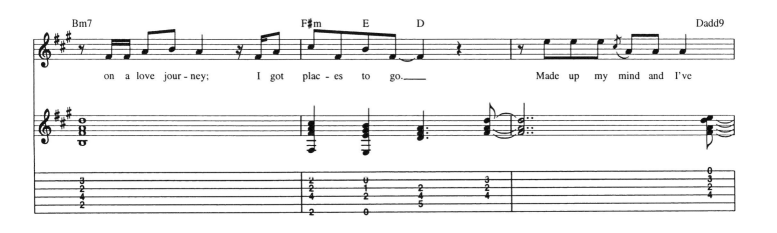

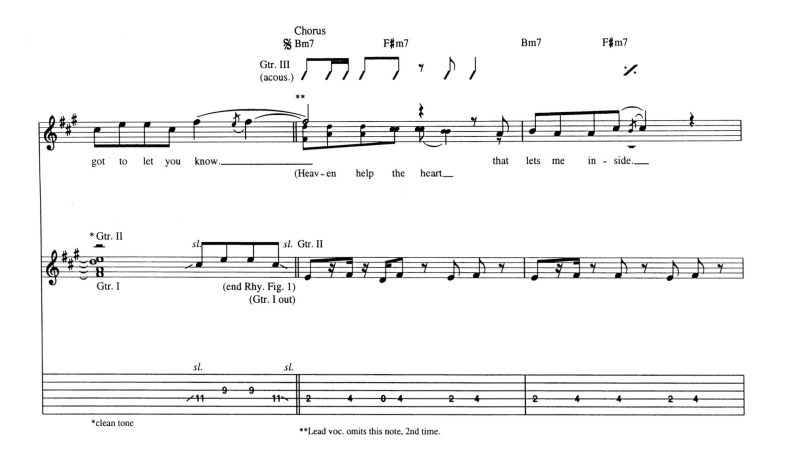

*clean tone

**Lead voc. omits this note, 2nd time.

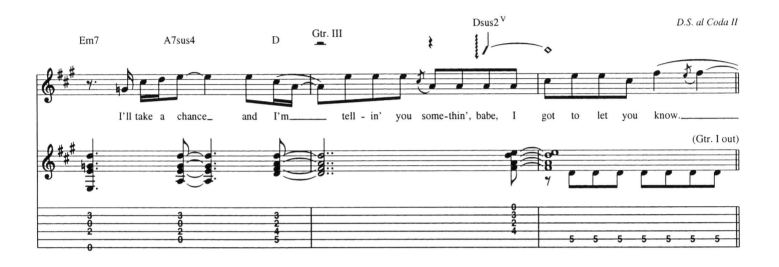

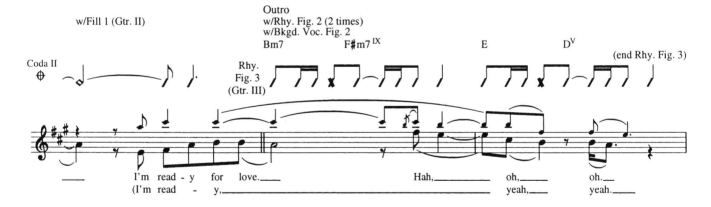

I BELONG TO YOU

Words and Music by
Lenny Kravitz

*Synth. arr. for gtr.

**Bass arr. for gtr.

You pick__ me up__ from a - bove. Your un - con - di - tion - al love

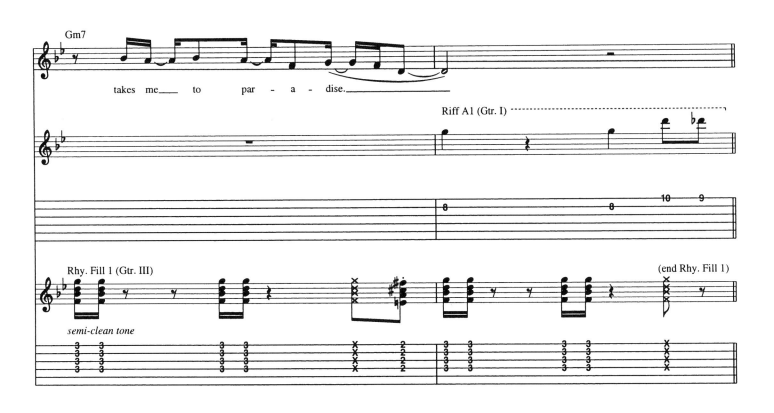

takes me__ to par - a - dise.__

I be - long__ to you,__ and you,

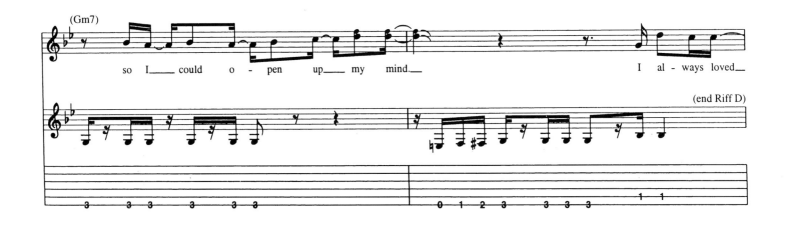

(Gm7)

so I___ could o - pen up___ my mind.___

(end Riff D)

I al - ways loved___

3 3 3   3   3 3   0 1 2 3   3 3 3   1 1

w/Riff D
Cm7
Rhy.
Fig. 2
(Gtr. IV)

___ you from___ the start,___ but I could___ not fig - ure out___ that I had___

(end Rhy. Fig. 2)

Gm7

___ to do___ it ev - er - y day.___ So I put___

w/Rhy. Fig. 2
Cm7

___ a - way___ the fight.___ Now I'm gon - na live___ my life___ giv - ing you___

w/Rhy. Fill 1
Gm7

w/Riff A1

___ the most___ in ev - er - y way.___ Oh,___

Chorus
w/Riff C (4 times)
w/Rhy. Figs. 1 & 1A (both 2 times)
Cm7

Gm7

I be - long___ to you,___ and you, you be - long___ to me,___ too.___
And you...

You make my life com-plete. You make me feel so sweet.

Oh, I be-long to you, I be-long to you, and you, you...

you be-long to me, too. You make my life com-plete. Oh.

You make me feel so sweet.

Guitar solo
w/Riff C (2 times)
w/Rhy. Figs. 1 & 1A
Cm7
Gtr. V

clean tone w/delay

Ba, da, da, ba, ba. Ba, da, da, ba, ba. Ba, da, da,

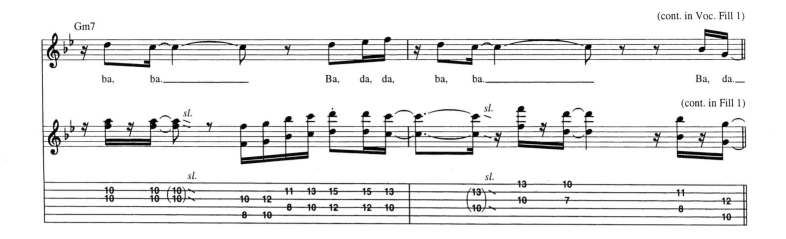

(cont. in Voc. Fill 1)

ba,   ba.   Ba,   da,   da,   ba,   ba.   Ba,   da.

(cont. in Fill 1)

sl.

Chorus
w/Riff C (1¾ times)
w/Rhy. Figs. 1 & 1A
1st time w/Voc. Fill 1 and Fill 1

I   be-long   to   you,   and   you,   you   be-long   to   me,   too.

I   be-long   to   you,   and   you...

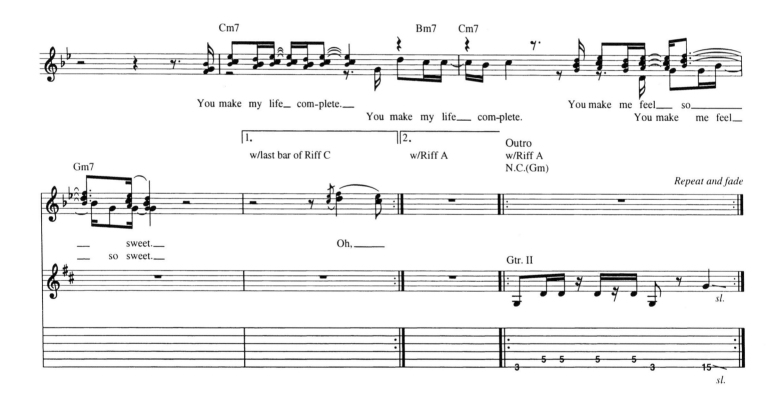

You make my life_ com-plete._   You make me feel_ so_

You make my life_ com-plete.   You make me feel_

|1.
w/last bar of Riff C

||2.
w/Riff A

Outro
w/Riff A
N.C.(Gm)

Repeat and fade

_   sweet._   Oh,_

_   so sweet._

Gtr. II

Voc. Fill 1

Fill 1 (Gtr. V)
(Gtr. V out)
sl.

sl.

BELIEVE

Words by Lenny Kravitz

Music by Lenny Kravitz
and Henry Hirsch

*Rhy. Fig. 1A is Rhy. Fig. 1 plus Rhy. Fill 1. Substitute open A (5th) string
for first eighth note of Rhy. Fig. 1 each time.

Additional Lyrics

2. The Son of God is in our face,
   Offering us eternal grace.
   If you want it, you got to believe.
   'Cause being free is a state of mind.
   We'll one day leave this all behind.
   Just put your faith in God, and one day you'll see, yeah. *(To Chorus)*

3. The future's in our present hands.
   Let's reach right in. Let's understand.
   If you want it, you got to believe, yeah. *(To Chorus)*

LET LOVE RULE

Words and Music by
Lenny Kravitz

*1st note of this bar is tied, not struck.

*distortion on.

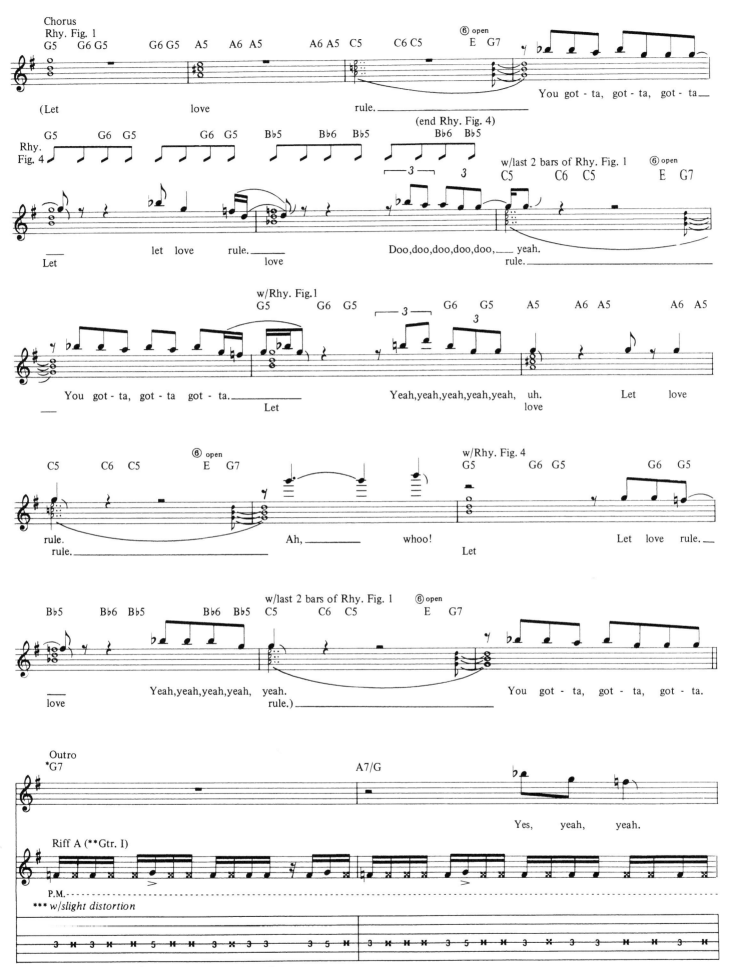

Doo-bie, doo-bie, doo-bie, doo-bie, doo, yeah,

(end Riff A)

semi-harm.

*Play note in parentheses first time only.

*w/Riff A

yeah, yeah. You got to, yeah. Whee!__

*Play Riff A w/variations when recalled.

w/Fill 2

You got-ta, got-ta, got-ta, got-ta, yeah.__

w/Fill 3

Yeah, yeah, yeah, yeah, yeah, yeah. Let love rule.__

w/Fill 4 w/Riff A

Fill 2
P.M.

Fill 3
P.M.

Fill 4
P.M.

BLACK VELVETEEN

Words and Music by
Lenny Kravitz

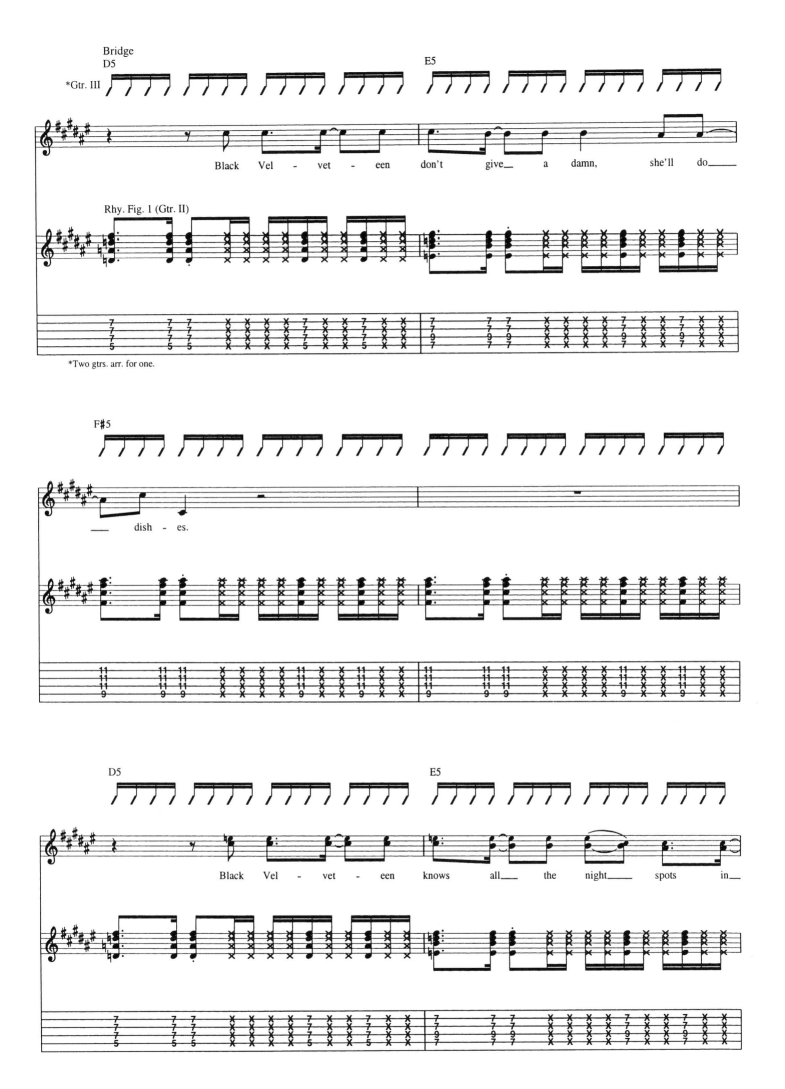

F#5

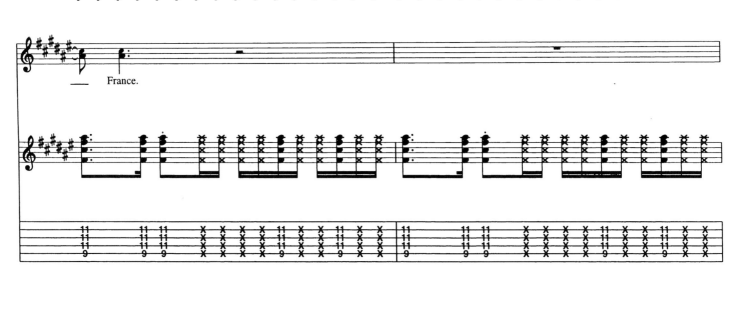

France.

D5   E5

Rhy.
Fig. 1A

Black Vel - vet - een's   cat   smells   like_____   straw - ber -

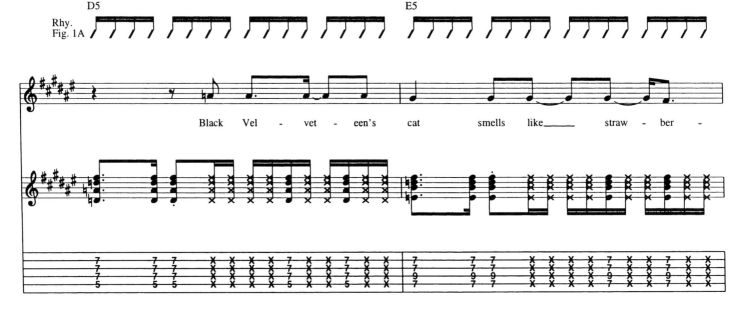

B5

ry   kit - tens.

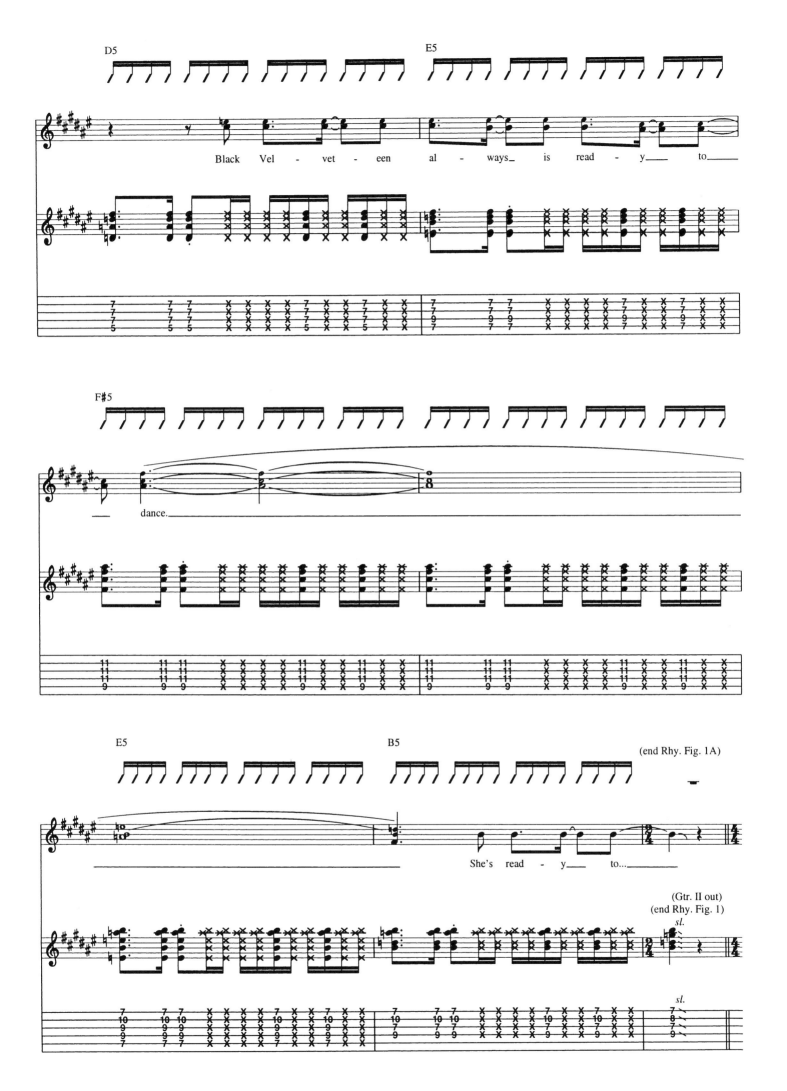

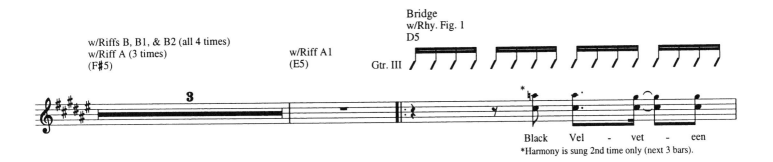

w/Riffs B, B1, & B2 (all 4 times)
w/Riff A (3 times)
(F#5)

w/Riff A1
(E5)

Bridge
w/Rhy. Fig. 1
D5

Gtr. III

*Harmony is sung 2nd time only (next 3 bars).

Black Vel - vet - een

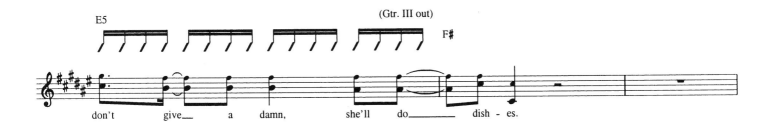

E5

(Gtr. III out)

F#

don't give a damn, she'll do dish - es.

D5

E5

(Gtr. III out)

Gtr. III

Black Vel - vet - een knows all the night spots in

F# w/Rhy. Fig. 1A
D5

E5

France. Black Vel - vet - een's cat smells like straw - ber -

B5

D5

E5

ry kit-tens. Black Vel - vet - een al - ways is read - y to

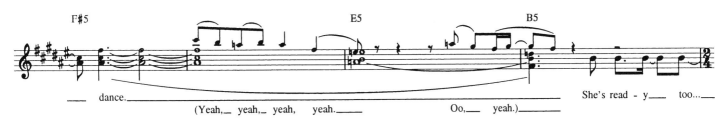

F#5

E5

B5

dance. (Yeah, yeah, yeah, yeah. Oo, yeah.) She's read - y too...

Chorus
w/Riff A and Rhy. Fig. 2 (both 7 times)
F#5

Black Vel - vet - een, sim - ple and clean. Oh, what a

bad ma - chine - a. Black Vel - vet - een, sup - ple and

w/Riff A1 and Rhy. Fig. 2A
E5

w/Riff A and Rhy. Fig. 1 (both 7 times)
F#5

lean, the twen - ty - first cen - t'ry dream - a. Black Vel - vet -

een, sim - ple and clean. Oh, what a bad ma - chine - a. Black Vel - vet -

w/Riff A1 and Rhy. Fig. 2A
E5

een, sup - ple and lean, the twen - ty - first cen - t'ry dream - a.

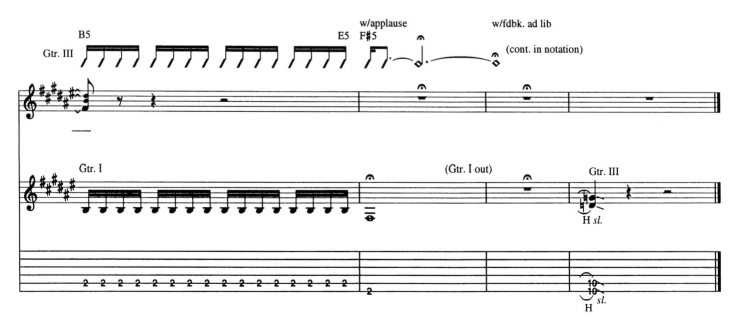

TABLATURE: A six-line staff that graphically represents the guitar fingerboard. By placing a number on the appropriate line, the string and the fret of any note can be indicated. For example:

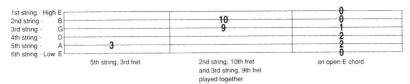

| 1st string - High E |
| 2nd string - B |
| 3rd string - G |
| 4th string - D |
| 5th string - A |
| 6th string - Low E |

5th string, 3rd fret   2nd string, 10th fret   an open E chord
                            and 3rd string, 9th fret
                            played together

Definitions for Special Guitar Notation

BEND: Strike the note and bend up a half step (one fret).

BEND: Strike the note and bend up a whole step (two frets).

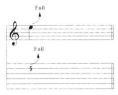

BEND AND RELEASE: Strike the note and bend up a half (or whole) step, then release the bend back to the original note. All three notes are tied; only the first note is struck.

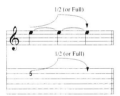

PRE-BEND: Bend the note up a half (or whole) step, then strike it.

PRE-BEND AND RELEASE: Bend the note up a half (or whole) step, strike it and release the bend back to the original note.

UNISON BEND: Strike the two notes simultaneously and bend the lower note to the pitch of the higher.

VIBRATO: Vibrate the note by rapidly bending and releasing the string with a left-hand finger.

WIDE OR EXAGGERATED VIBRATO: Vibrate the pitch to a greater degree with a left-hand finger or the tremolo bar.

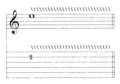

SLIDE: Strike the first note and then with the same left-hand finger move up the string to the second note. The second note is not struck.

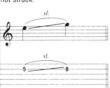

SLIDE: Same as above, except the second note is struck.

SLIDE: Slide up to the note indicated from a few frets below.

HAMMER-ON: Strike the first (lower) note, then sound the higher note with another finger by fretting it without picking.

PULL-OFF: Place both fingers on the notes to be sounded. Strike the first (higher) note, then sound the lower note by pulling the finger off the higher note while keeping the lower note fretted.

TRILL: Very rapidly alternate between the note indicated and the small note shown in parentheses by hammering on and pulling off.

TAPPING: Hammer ("tap") the fret indicated with the right-hand index or middle finger and pull off to the note fretted by the left hand.

NATURAL HARMONIC: With a left-hand finger, lightly touch the string over the fret indicated, then strike it. A chime-like sound is produced.

ARTIFICIAL HARMONIC: Fret the note normally and sound the harmonic by adding the right-hand thumb edge or index finger tip to the normal pick attack.

A.H. pitch: E

TREMOLO BAR. Drop the note by the number of steps indicated, then return to original pitch.

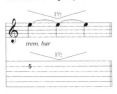

PALM MUTE: With the right hand, partially mute the note by lightly touching the string just before the bridge.

MUFFLED STRINGS: Lay the left hand across the strings without depressing them to the fretboard; strike the strings with the right hand, producing a percussive sound.

PICK SLIDE: Rub the pick edge down the length of the string to produce a scratchy sound.

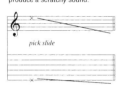

TREMOLO PICKING: Pick the note as rapidly and continuously as possible.

RHYTHM SLASHES: Strum chords in rhythm indicated. Use chord voicings found in the fingering diagrams at the top of the first page of the transcription.

SINGLE-NOTE RHYTHM SLASHES: The circled number above the note name indicates which string to play. When successive notes are played on the same string, only the fret numbers are given.

RECORDED VERSIONS®
The Best Note-For-Note Transcriptions Available

AUTHENTIC TRANSCRIPTIONS WITH NOTES AND TABLATURE

00690603	Aerosmith – O Yeah! Ultimate Hits	$29.99
00690178	Alice in Chains – Acoustic	$22.99
00694865	Alice in Chains – Dirt	$19.99
00694925	Alice in Chains – Jar of Flies/Sap	$19.99
00691091	Alice Cooper – Best of	$24.99
00690958	Duane Allman – Guitar Anthology	$29.99
00694932	Allman Brothers Band – Volume 1	$29.99
00694933	Allman Brothers Band – Volume 2	$27.99
00694934	Allman Brothers Band – Volume 3	$29.99
00690945	Alter Bridge – Blackbird	$24.99
00123558	Arctic Monkeys – AM	$24.99
00214869	Avenged Sevenfold – Best of 2005-2013	$29.99
00690489	Beatles – 1	$24.99
00694929	Beatles – 1962-1966	$27.99
00694930	Beatles – 1967-1970	$29.99
00694880	Beatles – Abbey Road	$19.99
00694832	Beatles – Acoustic Guitar	$27.99
00690110	Beatles – White Album (Book 1)	$19.99
00692385	Chuck Berry	$24.99
00147787	Black Crowes – Best of	$24.99
00690149	Black Sabbath	$19.99
00690901	Black Sabbath – Best of	$22.99
00691010	Black Sabbath – Heaven and Hell	$24.99
00690148	Black Sabbath – Master of Reality	$19.99
00690142	Black Sabbath – Paranoid	$19.99
00148544	Michael Bloomfield – Guitar Anthology	$24.99
00158600	Joe Bonamassa – Blues of Desperation	$24.99
00198117	Joe Bonamassa – Muddy Wolf at Red Rocks	$24.99
00283540	Joe Bonamassa – Redemption	$24.99
00358863	Joe Bonamassa – Royal Tea	$24.99
00690913	Boston	$22.99
00690491	David Bowie – Best of	$22.99
00286503	Big Bill Broonzy – Guitar Collection	$19.99
00690261	The Carter Family Collection	$19.99
00691079	Johnny Cash – Best of	$24.99
00690936	Eric Clapton – Complete Clapton	$34.99
00694869	Eric Clapton – Unplugged	$24.99
00124873	Eric Clapton – Unplugged (Deluxe)	$29.99
00138731	Eric Clapton & Friends – The Breeze	$24.99
00139967	Coheed & Cambria – In Keeping Secrets of Silent Earth: 3	$24.99
00141704	Jesse Cook – Works, Vol. 1	$19.99
00288787	Creed – Greatest Hits	$22.99
00690819	Creedence Clearwater Revival	$27.99
00690648	Jim Croce – Very Best of	$19.99
00690572	Steve Cropper – Soul Man	$22.99
00690613	Crosby, Stills & Nash – Best of	$29.99
00690784	Def Leppard – Best of	$24.99
00694831	Derek and the Dominos – Layla & Other Assorted Love Songs	$24.99
00291164	Dream Theater – Distance Over Time	$24.99
00278631	Eagles – Greatest Hits 1971-1975	$22.99
00278632	Eagles – Very Best of	$39.99
00690515	Extreme II – Pornograffiti	$24.99
00150257	John Fahey – Guitar Anthology	$24.99
00690664	Fleetwood Mac – Best of	$24.99
00691024	Foo Fighters – Greatest Hits	$24.99
00120220	Robben Ford – Guitar Anthology	$29.99
00295410	Rory Gallagher – Blues	$24.99
00139460	Grateful Dead – Guitar Anthology	$34.99
00691190	Peter Green – Best of	$24.99

00287517	Greta Van Fleet – Anthem of the Peaceful Army	$22.99
00287515	Greta Van Fleet – From the Fires	$19.99
00694798	George Harrison – Anthology	$24.99
00692930	Jimi Hendrix – Are You Experienced?	$29.99
00692931	Jimi Hendrix – Axis: Bold As Love	$24.99
00690304	Jimi Hendrix – Band of Gypsys	$27.99
00694944	Jimi Hendrix – Blues	$29.99
00692932	Jimi Hendrix – Electric Ladyland	$27.99
00660029	Buddy Holly – Best of	$24.99
00200446	Iron Maiden – Guitar Tab	$34.99
00694912	Eric Johnson – Ah Via Musicom	$24.99
00690271	Robert Johnson – Transcriptions	$27.99
00690427	Judas Priest – Best of	$24.99
00690492	B.B. King – Anthology	$29.99
00130447	B.B. King – Live at the Regal	$19.99
00690134	Freddie King – Collection	$22.99
00327968	Marcus King – El Dorado	$22.99
00690157	Kiss – Alive	$19.99
00690356	Kiss – Alive II	$24.99
00291163	Kiss – Very Best of	$24.99
00345767	Greg Koch – Best of	$29.99
00690377	Kris Kristofferson – Guitar Collection	$22.99
00690834	Lamb of God – Ashes of the Wake	$24.99
00690525	George Lynch – Best of	$29.99
00690955	Lynyrd Skynyrd – All-Time Greatest Hits	$24.99
00694954	Lynyrd Skynyrd – New Best of	$24.99
00690577	Yngwie Malmsteen – Anthology	$29.99
00694896	John Mayall with Eric Clapton – Blues Breakers	$19.99
00694952	Megadeth – Countdown to Extinction	$24.99
00276065	Megadeth – Greatest Hits: Back to the Start	$27.99
00694951	Megadeth – Rust in Peace	$27.99
00690011	Megadeth – Youthanasia	$24.99
00209876	Metallica – Hardwired to Self-Destruct	$24.99
00690646	Pat Metheny – One Quiet Night	$24.99
00102591	Wes Montgomery – Guitar Anthology	$27.99
00691092	Gary Moore – Best of	$27.99
00694802	Gary Moore – Still Got the Blues	$24.99
00355456	Alanis Morisette – Jagged Little Pill	$22.99
00690611	Nirvana	$24.99
00694913	Nirvana – In Utero	$22.99
00694883	Nirvana – Nevermind	$19.99
00690026	Nirvana – Unplugged in New York	$19.99
00265439	Nothing More – Tab Collection	$24.99
00243349	Opeth – Best of	$22.99
00690499	Tom Petty – Definitive Guitar Collection	$24.99
00121933	Pink Floyd – Acoustic Guitar Collection	$27.99
00690428	Pink Floyd – Dark Side of the Moon	$22.99
00244637	Pink Floyd – Guitar Anthology	$24.99
00239799	Pink Floyd – The Wall	$27.99
00690789	Poison – Best of	$22.99
00690925	Prince – Very Best of	$24.99
00690003	Queen – Classic Queen	$24.99
00694975	Queen – Greatest Hits	$25.99
00694910	Rage Against the Machine	$24.99
00119834	Rage Against the Machine – Guitar Anthology	$24.99
00690426	Ratt – Best of	$24.99
00690055	Red Hot Chili Peppers – Blood Sugar Sex Magik	$19.99

00690379	Red Hot Chili Peppers – Californication	$22.99
00690673	Red Hot Chili Peppers – Greatest Hits	$24.99
00690852	Red Hot Chili Peppers – Stadium Arcadium	$29.99
00690511	Django Reinhardt – Definitive Collection	$24.99
00690014	Rolling Stones – Exile on Main Street	$24.99
00690631	Rolling Stones – Guitar Anthology	$34.99
00323854	Rush – The Spirit of Radio: Greatest Hits, 1974-1987	$22.99
00173534	Santana – Guitar Anthology	$29.99
00276350	Joe Satriani – What Happens Next	$24.99
00690566	Scorpions – Best of	$24.99
00690604	Bob Seger – Guitar Collection	$24.99
00234543	Ed Sheeran – Divide*	$19.99
00691114	Slash – Guitar Anthology	$34.99
00690813	Slayer – Guitar Collection	$24.99
00690419	Slipknot	$22.99
00316982	Smashing Pumpkins – Greatest Hits	$24.99
00690912	Soundgarden – Guitar Anthology	$24.99
00120004	Steely Dan – Best of	$27.99
00322564	Stone Temple Pilots – Thank You	$22.99
00690520	Styx – Guitar Collection	$22.99
00120081	Sublime	$22.99
00690531	System of a Down – Toxicity	$19.99
00694824	James Taylor – Best of	$19.99
00694887	Thin Lizzy – Best of	$22.99
00253237	Trivium – Guitar Tab Anthology	$24.99
00690683	Robin Trower – Bridge of Sighs	$19.99
00156024	Steve Vai – Guitar Anthology	$39.99
00660137	Steve Vai – Passion & Warfare	$29.99
00295076	Van Halen – 30 Classics	$29.99
00690024	Stevie Ray Vaughan – Couldn't Stand the Weather	$22.99
00660058	Stevie Ray Vaughan – Lightnin' Blues 1983-1987	$29.99
00217455	Stevie Ray Vaughan – Plays Slow Blues	$24.99
00694835	Stevie Ray Vaughan – The Sky Is Crying	$24.99
00690015	Stevie Ray Vaughan – Texas Flood	$22.99
00694789	Muddy Waters – Deep Blues	$27.99
00152161	Doc Watson – Guitar Anthology	$24.99
00690071	Weezer (The Blue Album)	$22.99
00237811	White Stripes – Greatest Hits	$24.99
00117511	Whitesnake – Guitar Collection	$24.99
00122303	Yes – Guitar Collection	$24.99
00690443	Frank Zappa – Hot Rats	$22.99
00121684	ZZ Top – Early Classics	$27.99
00690589	ZZ Top – Guitar Anthology	$24.99

COMPLETE SERIES LIST ONLINE!

HAL•LEONARD®
www.halleonard.com

Prices and availability subject to change without notice.
*Tab transcriptions only.

0622
272